Newcastle: Past and Present
Millennium Edition

Geoff Phillips

Published by G P Electronic Services
87 Willowtree Avenue, Durham City, DH1 1DZ.
Tel: 0191 384 9707
Email: geoff1946@aol.com
Website: www.gpelectronicservices.co.uk

First edition of Newcastle: Past and Present was published in 1990
The Special Edition was published in 1994

ISBN 0 9522480 7 7

Front cover design by Geoff Phillips
Main text, interior design, typesetting,
and graphics by Geoff Phillips.

Modern photographs by Craig Oliphant and Geoff Phillips

Printed by: Blamire Printers, Ferryhill, Co Durham

Acknowledgments:

Many thanks go to:
Christopher Fenwick for allowing me to use some of the photographs from the Fenwick Collection and checking the text of the Fenwick's store story.
My life long friend Bill Frain for his encouragement, and for posing for one of the photographs.
Mike Greatbatch of the Ouseburn Trust for his genuine enthusiasm towards this book and helping with its promotion.
Dilys Harding for allowing me to use some photographs from the City Library's massive archives.
David Lovie, Heritage Officer of Newcastle's Grainger Town Project, for writing the Foreword and for making valuable contributions to the text accompanying each photograph.
Graeme Norman, of the Photo Shop in Durham for his help and advice on photographic techniques.

Special thanks go to my wife June for painstakingly checking the text.

Details and pictures from other books by Geoff Phillips
may be seen at our website
http://on-tyne.north-east.co.uk/History/tyneside-pp.asp

Bibliography:

A History of Newcastle-on-Tyne - R J Charleton , 1893.
The Buildings of Grainger Town - David Lovie, 1997.
Northern City: An Architectural History of Newcastle upon Tyne - Lynn Pearson, 1996.
Newcastle upon Tyne - Peter Winter, David Milne, Jonathan Brown, Alan Rushworth.
Newcastle upon Tyne: Its growth and Achievements - S Middlebrook, 1950.
What's in a Name - Anna Flowers, Maria Hoy, 1992.
Eighteenth Century Newcastle - P M Horsley, 1971
Newcastle - Frank Graham (revised edition 1995).

Newcastle: Past and Present
Millennium Edition

Newcastle upon Tyne as it used to be in the late 19th century
and early 20th century, compared with the present day

Geoff Phillips

Foreword by David Lovie -
Heritage Officer at Newcastle's Grainger Town Project

Pictures and Words

If, as we say, "one picture is worth a thousand words", then any single one of the photographs of Newcastle from the Jack Phillips Collection can inspire at least a thousand rich and telling words. But, what if we then couple the picture with another one taken at the same place 65 years on, and then link that one with a third taken a further 30 years later? Well, we get much more than a few thousand words - instead we get a precious glimpse into the turning world of time and change, which gives each chosen location its own special mystery and unique sense of place. To be able to stand in one place, as still as the photographers, and watch what are nothing less than frozen moments of time pass in succession before our very eyes, has a deep fascination for most of us. We are provided with startling insights into our changing townscape and into the human societies that over the years have used and abused it. In fact, to be privy to exactly what has gone before enables us to appreciate our present surroundings in an entirely new and refreshing way. By bringing these past worlds to our present attention in such an orderly and accessible way, Geoff Phillips has done us all a great service.

Grainger Town : Past

Over half of the 70 locations illustrated in this invaluable book of photographs lie within the very heart of our great city of Newcastle, a heart that since 1991 has come to be known as Grainger Town. Although Grainger Town contains significant chunks of medieval, 18th Century and Victorian Newcastle, it got its name from the massive building development that builder Richard Grainger carried out between 1834 and 1842. It was a colossal undertaking, achieved in seven incredibly short years and without the help of the mighty building machinery we use nowadays. But, once complete, its magnificence rivalled similar - but earlier - developments in Edinburgh or Bath. In fact, Prime Minister Gladstone described Grey Street, in his 1862 diary, as "our best modern street". Grainger's basic building unit was the stone terraced house over a shop. But what terraces they are!

All the houses are grandly set away from the street noise above fine shops and the stonework is tricked out to form huge palace-like terraces with prominent end wings and protruding central pavilions, sometimes with massive decorated columns and other times with delicately curved street corners. Everywhere the wide street vistas are cleverly terminated by a huge column as in Grey and Grainger Streets or by terrace pavilions or bow-fronted pubs as in Nun and Nelson Streets. In spite of the speed of building, all is carefully composed. The unfortunate neglect and slow decay of this fine legacy over the years is chronicled by many of Geoff Phillips' published photographs.

Grainger Town : Present (and Future)

But, all is not lost. In 1997 Newcastle City Council, with several enthusiastic local and national partners, established a Grainger Town Company, supported by a 14 strong regeneration team, all charged with the considerable task of bringing Grainger Town back to viable life. This was to be achieved within six years - one less than Richard Grainger took to build his legacy - by encouraging new business and housing uses in vacant upper floors; by creating more employment; by repairing and improving buildings, shops and streets; and by introducing more cultural activities inside and outside the many handsome buildings of Grainger Town. In essence, the Project sets out to replace the doom and gloom of a run-down and decaying city quarter with both the electric buzz of a 24 hour European City and the leisurely pleasures of an all year round outdoor café society. Something of a challenging task.

We should, therefore, look forward to Geoff Phillips' next book as his photographs taken in the New Millennium will, no doubt, record and celebrate the improvements achieved by the Grainger Town Project, its partners and its many supporters. There is much to look forward to.

Contents

Newcastle: Past and Present - Millennium Edition

It's nearly two thousand years since a Roman soldier decided that the place we now call Newcastle was a good spot to build a bridge across the River Tyne. The river was narrow here and the high land next to it was an ideal place to build a fort to guard the crossing. The bridge was called Pons Aelius (Aelius being the family name of the Emperor Hadrian). The year was about AD120 and Hadrian ordered a wall to be built from Pons Aelius across England to the west coast. The wall was expanded east to Wallsend (Segedunum) some time later. The fort at Pons Aelius accommodated several hundred soldiers whose brief was to defend the northernmost border of their empire from the marauding Scots tribes.

Now nearly 2000 years later, as we enter a new millennium, Newcastle upon Tyne is a city with a population of over 275,000 which boasts a rich culture and heritage. This book shows the City and its suburbs as it used to be in the late 19th century and early 20th Century along with modern photographs taken from the same spot. It is now ten years since the first edition of 'Newcastle: Past and Present' was published, yet in that relatively small span in time, many areas of the City have changed so much that an update of the modern photographs was seen as long overdue.

The Jack Phillips Photograph Collection

This book features photographs from my late father's collection of photographs of Newcastle upon Tyne as it was in days gone by. Some of the photographs date back to the 1840's which is when photography was in its infancy.

Jack Phillips was born in Bishop Auckland, Co Durham in 1910 and was one of a family of five brothers and sisters. His father was a postman with Bishop Auckland GPO and Jack followed in his father's footsteps by joining the Post Office as a telegraph boy in 1924. In six years he graduated to postman and worked at post offices in Stockton, Thornaby, and Whitley Bay for fourteen years until he was retired from the GPO due to a duodenal ulcer. He always regarded his imposed retirement as most unfair as his complaint did not affect his work to any significant degree. After working for the Home & Counties Tea Company for a while, in 1939 he was called up to join the Territorial Army at Gosforth Park as a motorbike despatch rider.

When the war was over, Jack took up a post as costing clerk with C A Parsons, the steam turbine manufacturer of Byker, a suburb of Newcastle upon Tyne. A few years later he married and lived in a flat on Shields Road in Byker. He took a great interest in the history of Newcastle and started collecting old photographs, sketches and historical notes on the City. His collection was greatly augmented when he was given a collection of rare prints of views of Newcastle by a retired doctor from Jesmond. The doctor had been a collector himself for many years and wanted his collection to be adopted by a serious enthusiast. Many of the prints were in poor condition and Jack arranged for them to be copied so that negatives were produced for further printing of the photographs.

In the 1950's and 1960's Jack spent many Sunday mornings walking around the streets of Newcastle, trying to discover the locations of the old photographs and, with the help of a photographer friend, he set about taking new photographs of the old views so as to produce a "then and now" pair of pictures. His old Newcastle photographs appeared regularly in the Newcastle Evening Chronicle newspaper and Northern Life magazine and he gave exhibitions of his collection at Harkers of Grainger Street and Lockhart's Neville Street restaurant for their diamond jubilee celebration in 1951. Displays of his photographs were often seen in the canteen of C A Parsons and he liaised closely with the staff of the local studies department of Newcastle upon Tyne's Central Library. He was often called upon to show parties of visitors around the historical parts of the city.

Jack Phillips died of cancer in February 1986 at the age of 75, leaving a unique pictorial record of the streets and buildings of Newcastle upon Tyne and its suburbs. I have prepared this book in memory of my father and so that many more people can view and enjoy some of the photographs from his collection.

Past and Present

One of the most fascinating aspects of Jack's collection was the past and present pairs of photographs where he attempted to replicate the same camera angles as the early shots, and wherever possible, include a point of reference which could be used as a link between the old and new photographs. When my father died I took an interest in his collection and realised that many of his "Present" views which had been taken in the 1950's and 1960's had changed again and were now "Old Newcastle". I decided to embark on phase three of the project and arranged to photograph the views again in the 1990's. In some cases all three photographs have been included in this presentation where the changes are pronounced. In two instances it has been possible to show four photographs of the same scene. In most cases there is an obvious link between the old and new photographs of the same view but sometimes the links are hard to find and searching for them adds to the reader's enjoyment of the book.

Replicating the same camera angles as the early photographs was not an easy task. The angle of the original camera lens was sometimes difficult to duplicate and in some cases a building occupied the spot where the original cameraman stood. In 1860 it was probably quite safe for the photographer to set up his tripod in the middle of the street but not in the 1990's. In order to get the correct angle for the 1990's photograph I sometimes risked life and limb waiting for a gap in the traffic and then stood in the middle of the street to take the photograph. Street signs, traffic lights and parked vehicles were also a problem which sometimes forced me to use a different vantage point.

The Jack Phillips Hawaiian Band at Gosforth Assembly Rooms in 1956

Jack Phillips the Musician

Jack's other passion was music. He played the Hawaiian guitar in his own band and supplied music for dancing at venues throughout the North-East in the 1940's and 50's. Jack is seen in the centre of the photograph above at the Gosforth Assembly Rooms supplying the music at a dinner dance for C A Parsons' transformer drawing office staff. Joe Hanley is playing the drums and Horsley Hall is on piano. Horsley is also a keen historian specialising in Tyneside's past.

A Walk Around Newcastle upon Tyne

If you are intrigued by the 'past and present' photographs in this book, you may wish to actually view the scenes for yourself. A walking route around the streets of Newcastle has been devised which enables the interested reader to see most of the views depicted, in the same order as they appear in the book. It should be pointed out that the walk is of considerable distance and some may wish not to cover the entire route in one day. Parts of the walk are not suitable for wheelchairs. A few views outside the city centre have been included in the book. These are not covered by the walk.

The route starts at the Tyne Bridge, the icon of Newcastle upon Tyne. If you are travelling to Newcastle by car you will find car parks all along the Quayside underneath the Tyne Bridge. Parking here will be impossible on a Sunday morning when the traditional Quayside market is held. View No 1, the Tyne Bridge, was taken from opposite the new law courts. The area close to the Tyne Bridge where the mini-roundabout is situated is called Sandhill. It was so-named because of a mound of silt or sand which would collect at this spot due to a tributary of the River Tyne called the Lort Burn which used to flow down the course of Grey Street and Dean Street. The large apsidal building in Sandhill is the Guildhall, the inside of which was built in 1658 and was the ancient centre of municipal government of the town, however, no part of the original building is visible from the outside.

The walking route now takes you north, up the curved street called Side. Before you reach the railway arch you will see the Side Gallery on your left which usually has interesting historical photographs on view, and is well worth a visit. Entrance is free and there are picture postcards of local scenes on sale. You then follow Side as it forks left and you come to view No 2 (descriptions of each view accompany the photographs). Continue up Side, cross St. Nicholas Street, and look east where you will see view No 3, the Black Gate and the Castle. The Black Gate was built in 1247, but the superstructure was modified late in the seventeenth century when it was converted into a dwelling. Walk through the Black Gate and turn to face the magnificent St Nicholas Cathedral and view No 4, Castle Garth. You are now in a very ancient part of the City which used to be part of the County of Northumberland. Continue under the railway bridge and on your right is the castle from which the city took its name. The new castle was built in 1080 by Robert Curthose, the eldest son of William the Conqueror. It was replaced between 1172 and 1177 by the present stone keep, built by Henry II. It is one of the finest examples of a square Norman keep in Britain. On your left is Moot Hall which was originally built for the County Courts of Northumberland between 1810-12. In between Moot Hall and the Bridge Hotel are Castle Stairs. By descending the Castle Stairs, you will find a very pleasant pathway which takes you under the High Level Bridge and round to view No 5, the High Level Bridge.

The walk now takes you north into the east end of Westgate Road. Continue west along Westgate Road and watch out for the Literary and Philosophical Society's building on the left, a Grecian style structure built in 1822 as a lecture and study centre for the Society's members. In 1879 Joseph Wilson Swan lectured there to a party of seven hundred northern engineers and scientists and demonstrated his new invention: the incandescent electric lamp.

Cross Orchard Street and then turn and look down Collingwood Street to see view No 6. It was along this street that the 'Blaydon Races' procession

Side 1811

passed in 1862. Continuing along Neville Street you will see George Stephenson's statue. The bronze statue, which was sculptured by John Lough, a native of Newcastle, stands on part of the site of the Hospital of the Blessed Virgin Mary of the Westgate which was removed in 1844 to make way for Neville Street. A few yards away from Stephenson's statue is an ancient stone pillar which is set into the corner of the modern building. This column is one of the gateposts of the Royal Grammar School founded by Alderman Thomas Horsley in the reign of Henry VIII. Among the scholars of the school were Admiral Lord Collingwood, Lord Eldon (Chancellor of England), and the poet Mark Akenside, whose greatest work was 'The Pleasures of the Imagination'.

Continuing along Neville Street you will pass the splendid Victorian architecture of the Central Railway Station, opened in 1850. As you pass the station you must look north to see view No 7, Bewick Street, named after the famous wood engraver, Thomas Bewick. Continue west along Neville Street and you will pass the International Centre for Life scheduled to open in 2000. With the Centre for Life on your left, turn left into

Marlborough Crescent and watch out for the Courtyard pub which is on the corner with Scotswood Road on the opposite side of Marlborough Crescent. View No 8 shows the Centre for Life taken from Scotswood Road. Walk west along Scotswood Road and you arrive at the new Redheugh Bridge which was completed in 1983 and opened by Diana, Princess of Wales. The Redheugh Bridge provides an alternative access to the west of the City along an upgraded thoroughfare - St James Boulevard (formerly Blenheim Street.) The new dual carriageway gives a convenient route right through to Gallowgate. View No 9(b) was taken from the west side of St James Boulevard and shows Newcastle's Grosvenor Casino. Continue towards the city centre along the boulevard and you will come to view No 10 which is looking west towards Newcastle's Discovery Museum. If you have time to spare, the museum is well worth a visit. It features exhibits about local industry, commerce, culture, and fashion and entrance is free.

Continue along St James Boulevard and turn right when you reach Westgate Road. As you walk east along Westgate Road notice the ornate Tyne Theatre and Opera House, home of the English Shakespeare Company. This theatre, built in 1867, is noted for its superb acoustics and almost complete set of working

The Central Station

Victorian stage machinery. Opposite the theatre is Bath Lane where the best remaining stretch of the medieval town walls may be seen along with Durham Tower which is one of 17 towers that used to exist around the walls. View No 11 was taken from Cross Street which is further east along Westgate Road. Further along Westgate Road is the junction with Clayton Street which is where views 12 and 13 were taken. Turn right into Clayton Street and slowly walk along looking south. As you approach Pink Lane, view No 12 will suddenly line up. Pink Lane follows the course of the old town wall. Retrace your steps back to Westgate Road to see view No 13 and then turn right into Westgate Road again. Before you reach Grainger Street look back up Westgate Road to see view No 14. Continue on to Grainger Street to see view No. 15, St. John's Church which is mainly 15th century. In a window on the north side of the church is the earliest known representation of Newcastle's Coat of Arms: three castles on a red background. Retrace your steps along Westgate Road, and cross over where you see the statue of Joseph Cowen, an important 19th century politician who owned the Newcastle Chronicle and built the Tyne Theatre on Westgate Road. Bear right into Fenkle Street to see view No 16. On your right are the Old Assembly Rooms. This fine building was erected in 1774-76 and was used by the gentry for masquerades, balls and other social functions which usually followed race meetings or court assizes. The interior of the building has been magnificently restored and decorated and is still used today as a banqueting suite. Walk up Fenkle Street, cross Clayton Street and continue until you arrive at the wonderful Georgian architecture of Charlotte Square.

A narrow cobbled lane called Friars leads you to Blackfriars (view No 17). Many English kings used Blackfriars as a lodging house and in 1334 Edward Baliol, the illustrious King of Scotland, got down on his knees at Blackfriars to pay homage to Edward III, King of England. After studying the site of the old friary of Blackfriars, turn right down Dispensary Lane onto Low Friar Street which emerges at the site of the White Cross on Newgate Street. The White Cross is recorded as early as 1410. In 1783 a market house with a clock tower and spire was built here, but all that remains today is a cross of white cobbled stones set into the mini roundabout. This can be seen in view No 18. Turn right into Newgate Street and continue south to the Bigg Market and views 19, 20, and 21. The Bigg Market is a

St John's Church

night-time 'Mecca' for Newcastle's party-people who frequent the many pubs, restaurants and nightspots here. Turn north again to see view No 22, Newgate Street. On your right is the re-sited memorial to Dr Rutherford, the 19th century Evangelist, doctor, and friend of the poor. Dr Rutherford was a temperance campaigner who proclaimed 'water is best!'

Continue north along Newgate Street and turn right into Clayton Street to see views 23 and 24. The walk now continues along Newgate Street and, as you pass the junction with Low Friar Street where the White Cross used to be, you will see view No 25. In order to see view No 26 you have to skirt along the tree-lined traffic island between Newgate Street and the multistorey car park. St. Andrews Street (formerly Darn Crook) connects Gallowgate to Newgate Street. Walk up St. Andrews Street and stand at the corner of Rosie's Bar to see view No 28. Return to the east side of Newgate Street and look South to see view No. 27, the Green Market. View No. 30, corner of Gallowgate and Percy Street, may be seen from roughly the same spot by turning and looking north-west. Cross over Newgate Street towards St. Andrews Church (reputed to be the oldest church in the City) whereupon you will see part of the old town walls which have been preserved at the north end of the Church grounds. Unless you are specifically looking for the remains of the town walls they can easily be missed, and indeed many of the residents of Newcastle may pass St. Andrew's Church every day without realising that part of Newcastle's medieval history is tucked away behind the church. Look across the mini-roundabout to see view No 29, the corner of Blackett Street and Percy Street. This area is now dominated by the exterior facade of the Eldon Square Shopping Centre.
Continue north into Percy Street and walk along the east side where, very soon, view No 31 will come into sight which is the corner of Gallowgate and Percy Street from another angle. Continuing northwards whilst looking across Percy Street will soon reveal views 32 and 33. Leazes

Arcade, was originally a Jewish synagogue but is now a comedy club called Hyena Cafe with student accommodation on the upper floors.

The route continues north along Percy Street which is straddled by Eldon Gardens, part of the Eldon Square shopping complex. Take time to visit this part of the shopping centre which has some very pleasing internal architecture. Eldon Gardens uses some of the items from the Edwardian Handyside Arcade which used to occupy the site.

Continue north and you will come to the Haymarket and view No 34, the site of the Farmer's Rest pub. The pub was demolished in 1995 to make way for a major extension to Marks and Spencer's store. The Haymarket also boasts a new bus station. Cross Percy Street and enter the new bus station. Walk north past the bus stands and you will see view No 35, which is now dominated by the circular Haymarket Metro station. It was here, beneath the Boer War memorial angel, that many a courting couple arranged to meet before sampling Newcastle's night life during the 1960's. On the left is the Callers Clock, presented to the City by Callers, 'the home of good furnishing', to celebrate their 75th anniversary, 1897 - 1972.

View No 36 looks south back down Percy Street and on the left is the Haymarket's new water feature based on heroic stone figures which surround the war memorial. Head towards St Thomas Church and the Civic Centre (as seen in view 35) and enjoy the beautiful grounds of the church which are used by many office workers from Newcastle's Civic Centre to relax in during their lunch break. View No 37, Barras Bridge, may be seen from these grounds by looking towards Newcastle Playhouse and the University of Newcastle.

St Andrew's Church

The Northumberland Road Mural

The route now takes you south down Northumberland Street which is the shopper's 'Mecca'. All of this street is now pedestrianised which makes it even more appealing to avid shoppers as they no longer fear being mown down by heavy traffic. Walking south you soon come to the junction with Northumberland Road and view No 38. A few yards along Northumberland Road you will find, set into the BHS department store's north facing wall, an interesting mural which details the most significant events in Newcastle's history. On the opposite side of the road is the spectacular steel, stone, and glass architecture of Cafe Pacific. View 41 may be seen by returning to Northumberland Street and looking south with Barclays Bank on your right. Continue south and the sparkling appeal of the retail stores of this well known street will be experienced, enhanced by first class street musicians. As you walk along, occasionally look up at the buildings on either side of the street and you will see some nice surprises.

Fenwick's store is situated opposite Lisle Street which is where view No. 39 was taken. Stop for tea in Fenwick's Terrace restaurant (view No 40) and then sample the finest retail experience in Newcastle, in the store's many departments. Back on Northumberland Street we head south towards Monument Mall on the right. Turn north to see view No 42. View No 43 was taken a little way further south on the opposite side of Blackett Street, underneath the wonderful gold clock of Northern Goldsmiths. View No 44 was taken from the balcony of the Odeon Cinema and shows the tremendous changes that have taken place at this corner of Northumberland Street and Blackett Street.

Walk west along Blackett Street and admire the new Caithness stone and granite paving which is part of the Grainger Town refurbishment programme. Views 45, 46, and 47 were taken around the Grey's Monument area. Retrace your steps to the junction of Blackett Street and Northumberland Street and carry straight on into New Bridge Street. After passing the City Library on your left you will come to the junction with John Dobson Street. Cross John Dobson Street and you will arrive at the Laing Art Gallery and a part of Newcastle which is to be made into a piazza style area with a blue mosaic carpet for pavement. The Laing Art Gallery was built in 1904 and alongside the Gallery is Higham Place, where Richard Grainger undertook his first major building venture. Look west to see view No 48. Opposite the Gallery are Portland Buildings which is home to the Newcastle Building Society. The buildings have been tastefully designed to harmonise with the Lying-in Hospital (a maternity hospital for the City's poor) which is in the centre of the development. The hospital was designed by John Dobson, and was

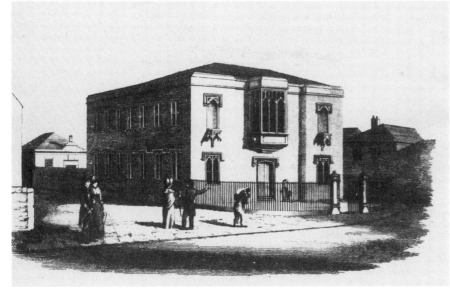

The Lying-in Hospital

built in 1826. For many years the BBC operated their North-East radio and television services from this building until they moved to new premises in Spital Tongues. With the Gallery behind you, walk south on John Dobson Street and you will come to Market Street. Turn left and then quickly right and you will see the Plummer Tower which was another of the towers on the town walls.

Rejoin Market Street and head west so that the large white building, Carliol House is on your right. Newcastle's main police station and magistrates' courts are on the left. The route now brings you to the junction of Market Street and Pilgrim Street. Cross Pilgrim Street and you will see view No 49 by looking north up Pilgrim Street. The Pilgrims would never have imagined this view of Pilgrim Street with masses of pre-cast concrete straddling the highway. Walk a few yards down Market Street and turn east to see view No 51. View No 50 is further west on Market Street where it intersects with Grey Street. Turn left and, as you walk southwards down Grey Street, admire the magnificent Theatre Royal, and take time to stop and marvel at the genius of the architects who designed this fine street. It is the gradual curve of Grey Street which adds to its appeal and puts it in the same class as London's Regent Street. Grey Street ends at its junction with Mosley Street. The continuation of Grey Street is Dean Street which eventually joins with Side. Turn left into Mosley Street and cross over the street. Mosley Street emerges at the Pilgrim Street roundabout where British Telecom's Swan House towers above a network of road intersections, motorway underpasses and pedestrian walkways. View No 52 shows the remarkable change that has occurred at this junction over the last 100 years. Turn right towards the Tyne Bridge to see view No 53. Descend the pedestrian walkway shown in view No. 53 and follow the signs marked 'City Road'.

In the centre of the Pilgrim Street pedestrian complex, underneath Swan House, is a re-creation of the interior of the Royal Arcade (which used to be on Pilgrim Street) which shows that there are still craftsmen today who can produce such fine work as shown in this re-creation, even though it was made in wood, and plaster. In the Swan House complex is a water sculpture by Raymond Arnatt as a memorial to Joseph Swan, it is entitled Articulate Opposites. The pedestrian ways eventually lead to what used to be the Holy Jesus Hospital which just escaped complete demolition during the 1960's when the Pilgrim Street roundabout complex was built. The hospital was built in 1681; part was used as a soup kitchen in 1880, but it is now vacant, awaiting a suitable new use.

Return to the pedestrian walkways and follow the signs to the All Saints Office Centre which leads to All Saints Church, built in 1786. It is a remarkable structure designed by David Stephenson and built on the site of All Hallows, which dates from at least 1286. We now arrive at a part of Newcastle that many people do not know exists. Descend Low Pilgrim Street and turn to see view No 54. We are now at the head of the very old streets of Akenside Hill and Dog Bank. This was one of the most densely populated areas of Newcastle in the early nineteenth century and was another route a traveller could take from the old Tyne Bridge to the town centre. Views 55 and 56 can be seen from either end of Dog Bank. Dog Bank descends to Broad Chare. Chares were the narrow lanes (of which there were about twenty) which connected Butcher Bank, and Pandon to the Quayside. At the foot of Dog Bank turn left, walk a few yards, and turn to see view No 57. Walk south along Broad Chare towards the new law courts and we come to Trinity House and the Trinity Maritime Centre. Broad Chare has been the

The facsimile of the Royal Arcade
Photo: Craig Oliphant

Trinity House Chapel and Hospital

home of the Master Mariners of the Newcastle Trinity House since 1505 although the existing buildings around the courtyard are mostly of eighteenth century origin. Access to the courtyard is only possible during office hours. The car park in front of Trinity House occupies an area of Newcastle known as Pandon and a tributary of the River Tyne called Pandon Burn used to flow through this part of town. Cross the car park behind the new law courts and you emerge at the Milk Market and Sandgate. A major rebuilding programme in the 1990's transformed this part of the City into an area of commerce, up-market housing, and places of entertainment. View No 58 shows the dramatic changes which have taken place, including the transformation of the Cooperative Warehouse to the Malmaison Hotel. Walk east along Sandgate and admire the new buildings. View 59 was taken further south towards the River Tyne.

Return to the Milk Market and look towards the Tyne Bridge to see view No 60. The early view shows the River Tyne spanned by only two bridges at this point. There are now a total of six bridges from Gateshead to Newcastle and another is under construction which will be a pedestrian bridge from the Quayside to the new cultural quarter on Gateshead's river bank. On the right are the newly constructed Law Courts. Head west along the Quayside towards the Tyne Bridge and Sandhill. This is the end of the walk.

Sandhill 1811

The Past and Present Photographs

On the following pages are the past and present photographs of Newcastle upon Tyne and its suburbs. In many cases there are links between the old and new views and they are quite good fun to find. For example, it's hard to believe that the two photographs of the Haymarket shown below were taken from the same spot, but notice that the stonework of the building on the extreme left is the same in both photographs. That building is the link. In some cases there are three or maybe four photographs taken from the same spot but at different times. There may be a link between all four photographs or there may be a link between (a) and (b), then a link between (b) and (c) and so on. Have fun finding the links. If you run into problems, the answers are given on pages 125 to 127.

Haymarket 1870

The old Haymarket pub may be seen on the right.

Haymarket 1993

The scene is now dominated by the Newcastle Breweries building. This is now used by the University of Newcastle.

Photo: Craig Oliphant

1(a) Quayside and Tyne Bridge 1928

Photo: Newcastle Libraries

The first bridge across the Tyne was built by the Roman Emperor Hadrian in about 121 AD. It was named Pons Aelius (bridge of Aelius) after the family name of the Emperor, and the Roman settlement adopted the same name. The Roman bridge survived for hundreds of years until invading tribes destroyed it. In the thirteenth century a bridge with shops and houses was built on roughly the same site as the present Swing Bridge. The medieval bridge was severely damaged by a terrible flood in 1771. The only bridge across the Tyne which was left standing was at Corbridge. The medieval Tyne Bridge was patched up with a wooden structure for a while until a new stone bridge was completed in 1781. This bridge was dismantled to make way for the Swing Bridge and when dredging work was underway, remains of the foundations for the previous bridges were found. The Swing Bridge was opened on 16 June 1876.

The present Tyne Bridge, opened in 1928, is the icon of Newcastle upon Tyne. Many people mistakenly believe that the Tyne Bridge was the model for the Sydney Harbour Bridge, to prove the design before the much larger Sydney construction was undertaken.

1(b) Quayside and Tyne Bridge 1999

Photo: Geoff Phillips

Construction work for the Sydney Harbour Bridge was started in January 1925 whereas building work on the Tyne Bridge did not commence until August 1925. The main contractor for the construction of the Tyne Bridge was Dorman Long and Co of Middlesbrough.

The photograph on the opposite page was taken in 1928 and shows the Tyne to be a busy port. Although motor vehicles were in service, many traders used horsepower to transport goods. In particular, a chain-horse may be seen behind the E M Younger lorry on the right. The horse's driver is sitting on the wall with his hands on his knees. A chain-horse was coupled by chains in front of the normal horse of a wagon to assist during the steep climb from the Quayside to the town centre.

The 1999 photograph above shows the Quayside Sunday market traders setting up their stalls in preparation for the day's trading. On the extreme right are the new law courts completed in 1990.

2(a) Side 1880

The street called Side was probably so-called because it ran up the side of the hill on which the castle was built. For centuries traffic crossing the old Tyne Bridge would have to negotiate this steep and narrow street to reach the centre of the city. In 1787 a new route was built called Dean Street which followed the course of the Lort Burn; a stream which ran into the River Tyne.

At the Head of Side, on the right, was a large house called the Meters Arms which is where Lord Collingwood was born in 1748. Young Cuthbert Collingwood was educated at the Royal Grammar School which was located on Westgate Road at the time. When his schooling was completed, his parents sent him to serve with the navy where he eventually became Admiral Collingwood. He fought in many famous battles and was rewarded with a peerage for his part in the Battle of Trafalgar.

2.(b) The Head of Side in 1876

2(c) 1952

In 1906, Milburn House replaced the old buildings on the right of the 1880 photograph. Milburn House was named after Alderman J D Milburn who bought the site and built these fine new offices after a huge blaze had destroyed the printing works of R Robinson and Co. Robinson's works and offices can be seen in the 1880 photograph. The buildings on the left are shored up and seem ready for demolition. There is an interesting link between the 1880 and 1952 photographs.

Photo: Jack Phillips

2(d) 1999

The shored-up buildings seen above do survive but are just out of camera shot in the 1999 photograph. St Nicholas Buildings in the centre of the photographs was erected shortly after the opening of the High Level Bridge in 1850. In 1996 the building was reduced to its historic facade only and a new structure with a higher roof was built behind.

Photo: Geoff Phillips

3(a) The Black Gate and Keep 1895

3(b) The Black Gate and Keep 1990's

Photo: Geoff Phillips

It was the year that every schoolchild remembers - 1066 when England's history took a turn. The Normans led by William the Conqueror defeated King Harold's army and England then became under Norman control. William found the Northumbrians a challenge, but in 1068 he paid a personal visit along with his best army. He destroyed the town near the bridge across the Tyne which was called Monkchester at the time. He also laid waste most of Northumbria. His eldest son Robert had been defeated by the Scots and on his return to England he stopped at what was left of Monkchester. Just like the Romans, the Normans realised this was a good spot to 'draw a border line on the map of their empire'. William left instructions with his son to build a wooden fort on the high ground above the bridge across the Tyne and the new castle gave the town a new name. The keep we see today was built from stone by Henry II between the years 1172 and 1177 and cost £892 18s 9d.

The Black Gate was the main entrance to the castle of Newcastle upon Tyne. It was built by King Henry III in 1248, about 70 years after the completion of the keep and other parts of the fortress. The upper section of the Black Gate was added in the early part of the 17th century when it was converted into a dwelling and took on its name.

The sketch on the opposite page was made from a position at the other side of the railway bridge. All Saints Church is shown on the right.

Since the 1895 view, the builder's yard on the right has been removed and the original castle moat has been dug and restored The Black Gate has been kept in good condition by the Society of Antiquaries who undertook major restoration work in the late nineteenth century. The Society now uses the building as a library and store. The keep is maintained by the City and is open to visitors. There are excellent views of Newcastle and Gateshead from its towers.

4(a) Castle Garth c1890

Castle Garth means castle yard. This photograph shows the part of the Garth leading to the Black Gate seen to the left of St Nicholas Cathedral. The Church of St Nicholas is believed to have been founded in 1091 by St Osmund, Bishop of Salisbury. The church was almost destroyed by fire in the thirteenth century.

Construction of the cathedral we see today began in the fourteenth century and was completed in 1448 with the addition of the distinctive lantern tower. The church gained cathedral status in 1882.

4(b) Castle Garth 1999

Photo: Geoff Phillips

In 1400 Henry IV drew up a charter which made Newcastle an independent county, but the keep and its grounds called Castle Garth were not part of the county. This area was owned by the Crown and was not under the jurisdiction of Newcastle. Consequently many villains would seek refuge from the authorities in Castle Garth. Queen Elizabeth I put a stop to this state of affairs with a charter in 1589 but the area was still part of the county of Northumberland.

If you wanted to run a business in Newcastle you had to be a member of the appropriate Trade Guild. Those who could not gain membership of a guild could set up shop in the Castle Garth and carry out their trade without fear of being closed down by the town's guilds. Many cobblers and tailors traded in Castle Garth before the area was bought by the City in 1812 when the new Moot Hall was built. Many of the old houses were demolished to build the Moot Hall and later to build the approaches to the High Level Bridge. The picture opposite was taken at the turn of the 19th century and shows the part of the Garth which remained. It passed the keep on the left (out of picture) and continued through to the Black Gate.

The Black Gate may be seen to the left of St Nicholas' lantern tower. The sign for Dog Leap Stairs may just be seen on the wall at the right. The stairs lead down to Side.

The 1999 photograph shows the cathedral undergoing some restoration. New gold-leaf is being applied to the weather vanes and some of the stone figures. The building on the right is Milburn House situated on Side.

My old friend Bill Frain is seen in approximately the same location as the seated figure in the 1890 photograph.

5(a) High Level Bridge 1895

In 1844 the completion of the Newcastle and Darlington railway resulted in a continuous rail link from London to Gateshead. North-East route trains could go no further north than Gateshead because of the wide and deep valley of the River Tyne. In July 1847, the link from Newcastle to Edinburgh was completed but the through route remained elusive. The railway company considered a railway bridge across the Tyne valley at Newcastle to be impractical and seriously considered building a bridge at Bill Point in Walker. If that had gone ahead, then the commercial centre of the region may have developed in that area instead of Newcastle.

It was Robert Stephenson , son of the famous railway engineer George Stephenson, who proposed the construction of a road/rail bridge at a high level linking Newcastle with Gateshead. The bridge was to be made from iron supported on stone columns and construction started in 1846. The most difficult part of the construction was the driving of piles into the river bed to support the stone columns. Two 1.5 ton steam hammers were used, however, the piles for the central column had to be driven through quicksand and water oozed from the sand as fast as it could be pumped

away. Pumping went on for months until the piles for the central column reached firm foundations.

The bridge was opened for traffic on 15th August 1849 but was officially opened by Queen Victoria in 1850. It stands 120 feet above low water level of the Tyne and is 1400 feet long.

The photograph above was taken in 1895 and shows the road entrance to the bridge at Newcastle; a toll was levied on road users of the bridge. The railway engine perched on top of the bridge is Stephenson's 'Billy' which was used to haul coal at Killingworth colliery. It is now housed in the Stephenson Railway Museum at Middle Engine Lane in the North-East suburbs of Newcastle.

Photograph 4(b) shown on the opposite page is the same scene in 1960 and shows my father Jack Phillips sitting on the railing.

In 1999 the bridge had given 150 years of service and an inspection was carried out by engineers who abseiled from the top of the bridge.

5(b) High Level Bridge 1960

Photo: Jack Phillips

5(c)   1999

6(a) Westgate Road / Collingwood Street 1904

6(b) Westgate Road / Collingwood Street 1953

Photo: Jack Phillips

6(c) Westgate Road / Collingwood Street 1999

Photo: Geoff Phillips

Westgate Road is to the right and Collingwood Street, named after Admiral Lord Collingwood, is straight ahead. The 1904 photograph shows the premises of the gun manufacturer W R Pape. Mr Pape was the inventor and patentee of breech loading guns and rifles. Pape eventually sold his premises to the Sun Insurance Company who demolished the building to construct the building seen in the two later photographs. Pape had new premises built in Pink Lane which still stand today.

On the left, in the 1904 photograph, Collingwood Buildings are under construction which includes a magnificent banking hall for Barclays.

Photograph (b) was taken in 1953 and shows the Sun Insurance building decorated with streamers to celebrate the Coronation of Elizabeth II. Although my father owned a car at the time, he often preferred to cycle to Newcastle, especially on a Sunday, in order to take photographs. His sporty bike can be seen leaning against the pole at the right of the photograph.

7(a) Bewick Street / Neville Street 1890

Bewick Street was named after the Northumberland-born wood engraver Thomas Bewick. He was born in Cherryburn, Mickley in 1753 and, on leaving school, was apprenticed to Ralph Beilby, Newcastle's only engraver, (at the time) at his workshop in St Nicholas' churchyard. Thomas Bewick revived the art of wood engraving and turned it into an art form, specialising in natural history. In 1797 he published the book, 'A History of British Birds' which featured his engravings. The book went on to six editions in Bewick's lifetime and it became the accepted standard reference work for ornithologists.

Bewick died in 1828 and was buried in Ovingham, Northumberland. There is a bust of Bewick in St Nicholas' churchyard and a statue of him above 43-45 Northumberland Street.

The photograph above shows Bewick Street in 1890. The gravestones in the foreground are not part of a graveyard but are the wares of Emley and Sons - Monumental Sculptors. The building on the extreme right is the old post office on Pink Lane. The building on the extreme left is Bewick House built in 1885. The photograph is rather blurred at the top left but it shows that the building only has two floors; three more floors were added in 1911.

7(b) Bewick Street / Neville Street 1999

Photo: Geoff Phillips

In the modern photograph the corner site is occupied by Gunner House built in the mid-sixties. In that era the ground floor was occupied by Bowers Restaurant - one of Newcastle's first 24 hour fast-food outlets. Scenes from the cult movie 'Get Carter' were filmed here in the late 1960's.

There are two links between the old and new photographs.

8(a) Scotswood Road

The above photograph shows Scotswood Road as it enters the west of Newcastle. Scotswood Road is mentioned in the Tyneside song 'Blaydon Races' and had the reputation of having dozens of pubs along its three mile length. Only two pubs remain: Rockie's Bar which used to be called The Marlborough, and The Courtyard which used to be called the Kings Head. The Kings Head may be seen on the corner to the left of the tram.

The area in the distance between the tram and the pub was Newcastle's sheep and pig market. Next to the two pedestrians on the right of the photograph can be seen the railings of Newcastle's cattle market and the cattle market keeper's house, designed by John Dobson, is the building with the clock tower.

The church with the tall, elegant spire is St Mary's Roman Catholic Cathedral.

8(b) International Centre for Life 1999

Photo: Geoff Phillips

Photograph (b) shows the International Centre for Life which is scheduled for completion in Spring 2000. It is a project of international status which explores life and how it works. It will bring together science and biotechnology, research and education, entertainment and ethics on a single site. The Centre will feature a Bioscience Centre, a Bioethics Forum, an Institute of Human Genetics and a Visitor Experience with an Education Superlab. The Centre's slogan is 'Celebrate Life' and builds on one of the greatest discoveries of all time - the secret of life itself - and explores how we became unique individuals, yet are related to daffodils and dinosaurs. The 1842 Market Keeper's house is retained as the centre-piece in the new square contained by the buildings of the Centre for Life.

The Blenheim Hotel was yet another pub on Scotswood Road which met its demise in the late 60's. The new St James' Boulevard, completed in the late 1990's, gives a direct route from the new Redheugh Bridge to Gallowgate and St James' Park, home of Newcastle United Football Club. Tower cranes used during the extensions to the stadium may be seen in the distance. There is a link between the old and new.

9(b) St James' Boulevard 1999

Photo:
Geoff Phillips

10(a) Sunderland Street / Blenheim Street   1966

Photo: Jack Phillips

The Queen Victoria pub in this early 19th century John Dobson suburb, was renamed the 'Black and White' in the 1980's and then 'Strings' before the bulldozers moved in. On the right of the 1999 photograph is the Discovery Museum which occupies the splendid 1899 CWS regional headquarters.

Photo: Geoff Phillips

10(b) St James' Boulevard   1999

11(a) Westgate Road / Lockhart's Cocoa Rooms 1895

This photograph, which was taken from Cross Street, shows Westgate Road where it intersects with Pink Lane (seen to the right). In the centre of the photograph is Lockhart's Cocoa Rooms which was one of a chain of budget priced restaurants. The restaurant chain was launched by Robert Lockhart when he opened his first restaurant in Liverpool in 1876. Mr Lockhart's policy was to give the best possible value for money and the restaurants soon became very popular throughout the country. They were seen by many as a welcome alternative to the drunken atmosphere of public houses and many a romance began over a cup of cocoa at The Rooms. In the early years the restaurants were closely associated with the temperance movement, in which Mr Lockhart himself was keenly interested. Lockhart's Cocoa Rooms were introduced to the City of Newcastle upon Tyne in 1891 by Robert Lockhart's son-in-law H Crawford Smith. Crawford Smith made Newcastle his home and became noted for his interest in philanthropy. He took particular interest in improving the welfare of poor children in the city and

supported Dr Barnardo's Homes and the Poor Children's Holiday Association. Crawford Smith was also a great supporter of the Temperance movement yet, ironically, he founded workingmen's clubs, although it is thought that in the early years the clubs were very different to what they are today and were more concerned with welfare than entertainment.

The restaurants continued to trade until the 1950's when the company was known as Lockhart Smith and Co. On Monday 17 December 1951 the company celebrated its diamond jubilee with a tea party in their Neville Street restaurant. My father was invited to provide a display of old Newcastle photographs from his collection on which this book is based. At that time Lockharts operated seven restaurants in Newcastle, one in South Shields and two in Sunderland.

The corner site on the above photograph is occupied by the Criterion public house which sports a handsome shaped gable end, once very fashionable in 17th and 18th century Newcastle.

11(b) 1951

The ornate building in the centre of the photograph to the left was built for the Lockhart organisation in about 1900. The inscription L & Co may be seen in the stonework. The corner site continued to be occupied by the Criterion public house until it closed in 1957.

Photo: Jack Phillips

11(c) 1999

Photo: Geoff Phillips

The view above shows John Knox Church designed by the famous architect John Dobson who designed many fine buildings in Newcastle upon Tyne and even better country houses in Northumberland. John Knox was a sixteenth century Scottish Protestant reformer who founded the Church of Scotland.

The John Knox Church was built on the site of the Pink Tower which was one of the 17 towers around the Town Wall.

Pink Lane, which leads to the Central Station, is seen to the left. This lane follows the line of the Town Wall.

12(b) Clayton Street / Pink Lane 1960

Photo: Jack Phillips

12(c) 1999

View (b) was taken in 1960 and the church has been demolished in 1896 to make way for Clarendon House, an Edwardian Arts and Crafts Temperance hotel.

View (c) is almost 40 years later and the shop on the corner still bears the name H Siger and Son.

Photo: Geoff Phillips

13(a) Clayton Street / Westgate Road 1915

This view shows the junction of Clayton Street and Westgate Road and looks north along Clayton Street. The Street, which was built in 1837, was named after John Clayton who was Newcastle's Town Clerk for 45 years in the nineteenth century. John Clayton helped to raise the vast sums of money required for Richard Grainger's ambitious plan to rebuild the city centre in the 1830's.

13(b) 1999

Photo: Geoff Phillips

14(a) Westgate Road

This view shows Westgate Road looking west. The Picture House, as seen in the previous 1915 photograph is being demolished to make way for a brand new cinema. In the 1950's, the cinema was a dancehall called the Majestic where popular bands of the time would entertain, but it's now a bingo hall.

14(b) 1990's

Photo: Craig Oliphant

15(a) Grainger Street 1890

This street was named after Richard Grainger who built many of Newcastle's finest streets and buildings. The medieval St. John's Church is on the right and the horse-drawn tram is heading towards the Central Station. The tram's hoarding is advertising the local pharmacist, Inman.

Photo: Geoff Phillips

15(b)
1999

16(a) Fenkle Street 1898

The photograph above shows Cross House to the left which was the home of Ralph Carr who founded the first bank in Newcastle in the 18th century. In the early 19th century it was used as the vicarage of St John's Church but was later re-fronted and used as business premises. The advertisement is for a show in Bull Park which was the former name of the Exhibition Park. The new Cross House shown below was built in 1911.

16(b) 1990's

Photo: Craig Oliphant

17(a) Blackfriars 1880

The order of Dominican or Black Friars was founded by a Spaniard called Dominic de Guzman (St Dominic). The Black Friars' first monastery in England was founded in Oxford in about 1221 and soon after another was set up in London. The friars settled in Newcastle upon Tyne in 1239 and were given land by 'three pious sisters' on which to build their monastery. Sir Peter Scott, the first Lord Mayor of Newcastle upon Tyne, is said to have funded the building of the monastery in the west of Newcastle just inside where the City Wall was later built. The Order was called Black Friars because they wore a black cloak with a hood covering a white cassock. People in Newcastle called them 'Shod Friars' as they wore footwear as opposed to the Franciscan Friars who went barefoot.

The friary in Newcastle was often visited by Kings of England when they were in the area and many resided there for a while bringing gifts of cloth, wine, corn and money. Edward Balliol paid homage to Edward III there in 1334.

After the dissolution of the monasteries, the friary at Newcastle was sold to the City Council who rented it to the nine main trade guilds: Bakers and Brewers, Butchers, Cordwainers, Fullers and Dyers, Saddlers, Skinners and Glovers, Smiths, Tanners, and Tailors. The photograph above, taken in 1880, shows two businesses in residence: Margaret Birkett - Provisions Dealer and G Willey - House Carpenter.

The photograph (b) on the opposite page was taken in the early 1950's when Blackfriars was falling into disrepair. My father took this picture: that's me with cap in hand.

By the 1960's the buildings were in a terrible state. The City Council gradually acquired all the property, restoration work began in 1975, and was completed in 1981. Blackfriars now houses several craft workshops, and the offices of the North-East Civic Trust.

17(b) Blackfriars c1951

Photo: Jack Phillips

17(c) 1999

Photo: Geoff Phillips

18(a) Newgate Street 1960's

Photo: Jack Phillips

In 1784 a market cross with a spire was constructed on Newgate Street opposite Low Friar Street. It replaced a former structure on the same site. The new cross, named the White cross, was ornamented on four sides with the coats of arms of the Mayor, magistrates, and Sheriff of the town. It was re-sited to a butcher market near High Bridge in 1808. When Richard Grainger rebuilt the centre of Newcastle, the White Cross did not form part of the plan and it disappeared. It is said, however, that the spire of the Cross was taken by Newcastle architect Dobson to become a feature in the garden of his house in New Bridge Street.

The photograph above shows the site where the White Cross stood; its actual position being denoted by a white cross painted on the road. View (b) shows the transition stage during the building of the Eldon Square Shopping Centre. The position of the White Cross in view (c) is now denoted by a cross of white cobbles in the mini-roundabout at the far right of 18(c).

The White Cross

18(b) 1970's

Photo: Jack Phillips

18(c) 1999

Photo: Geoff Phillips

19(a) Bigg Market

Bigg is a type of coarse barley which farmers brought to this part of the town to sell. The area gradually became a centre for trading in a wide range of goods.

The tall building on the right was Newcastle's Corn Exchange and town hall built 1858-63. There were many people opposed to its construction. In particular, John Dobson said, 'The hideous town hall would ruin the character of what might have been one of the finest streets in the kingdom.' Until 1838, the site of the town hall had been occupied by Middle Street and Union Street, and when they were demolished the Groat Market and Cloth Market faced each other across one of the finest views of St Nicholas Cathedral that Newcastle had ever seen. Nevertheless the town hall was built and when completed it attracted numerous literary criticisms.

A fine new Toon Hall, there's lately been built,
Te sewt mountybank dansors an' singors;
It's a sheym the way the munny's been spilt,

An wor Cooncil hez sair brunt their fingors;
For the room's dull an cawd, tee, an' ghostly an' lang,
An thor fine organ's not worth a scuddick;
An' if frae the gallery ye want te heer a fine sang,
Wey, ye might as weel be in a keel's buddick.

The Bigg Market, Cloth Market, and Groat Market area has always been a lively place with many inns and places of recreation. In 1882 there were 23 pubs, two theatres, 4 beerhouses and three breweries. One of the most famous pubs was The Wheatsheaf, better known as Balmbra's, where Geordie Ridley first sang his composition 'The Blaydon Races' in 1862.

The Bigg Market is still used today as a market on certain days of the week. At night the whole area comes alive as hundreds of revellers frequent the many bars, restaurants, and night clubs in the Bigg Market which is now world-famous for being the 'place to party'.

19(b) Bigg Market 1989

Photo: Craig Oliphant

19(c) 1999

Photo: Geoff Phillips

20(a) Corn Exchange and Old Town Hall, Bigg Market / Groat Market / Cloth Market

GROAT MARKET. LOOKING SOUTH
NEWCASTLE.

This view shows the old Corn Exchange and Town Hall built 1858-63. As well as the council offices, it housed a large concert hall, offices, shops, and the corn market. Yet another Lockhart's Cocoa Rooms faces the memorial fountain to the temperance reformer, Dr J H Rutherford who proclaimed 'Water is best'.

20(b) Bigg Market / Groat Market 1975

The Exchange and Town Hall were demolished in the early 1970's to make way for Stanegate House, seen being completed in this 1975 photograph.

The Rutherford memorial fountain was originally erected in St Nicholas square at the opposite end of the old Town Hall but was re-sited in the Bigg Market in 1902 to make way for the Queen Victoria Monument, (or perhaps it was sited in the Bigg Market to remind patrons of the many alehouses in the area of the 'dangers of drink'.)

The Bigg Market area was refurbished in the late 1990's and the memorial was re-sited again. It is now at the junction of the Bigg Market and Grainger Street.

Photo: Jack Phillips

20(c) Bigg Market / Groat Market / Cloth Market 1999

Photo: Geoff Phillips

21(a) Bigg Market / High Bridge 1899

The lane 'High Bridge' was named after the bridge over the Lort Burn, a tributary of the River Tyne, which ran down where Grey Street now stands.

On the left are the premises of M Young and Sons - Watchmaker; established in 1782. The original Bee Hive pub can be seen on the right.

Photo: Newcastle Libraries

21(b) Bigg Market / High Bridge 1999

The old Bee Hive pub was bought by Newcastle Breweries in 1896 and was rebuilt in 1902. Its upper floors are now occupied by student housing. The magnificent building on the left is Sunlight Chambers built 1901-02. It is beautifully decorated with figures working at harvest and industry. It too has been converted to student housing, with help from the Grainger Town Project.

Photo: Geoff Phillips

22(a) Newgate Street / Clayton Street 1911

In the centre of the photograph is the Empire Theatre which played host to many fine entertainers and acts. The Royal Philharmonic Orchestra played there in 1940, as did the Beatles in the early 1960's supported by the Everly Brothers. The theatre was closed in 1963 and demolished two years later. Although the Empire has now gone, the Rose and Crown pub continues to do business. The Chasley Hotel towers above the Newgate Shopping Precinct in the centre of the 1999 picture.

Photo: Geoff Phillips

22(b) 1999

23(a) Clayton Street East 1920

Richard Grainger's 1837 Clayton Street used to continue eastwards and join up with Blackett Street making a formal approach to the original Eldon Square that Richard Grainger had built between 1825 and 1831. It was built to the designs of John Dobson and Thomas Oliver, architects. At the end of Clayton Street was the fish market and the bird market and on the right of the picture is Grainger Market. Today, the buildings on the left form part of Eldon Square's Green Market. Clayton Street is now blocked off by more of the Square just beyond Nelson Street. Grainger Market is still in existence on the right.

23(b) 1990's

Photo:
Craig Oliphant

24(a) Clayton Street East 1915

This photograph was taken very near to the previous shot and shows the Cambridge public house in the centre. Further to the left, an employee of Mr Lockhart has stopped work for a while to observe the photographer, and the lady upstairs is also curious to know what is going on.

Although the upper floors of the market were originally built as separate three storey houses, little residential use now survives in these upper floors.

24(b) Clayton Street East 1990's

The main structure of the buildings is unchanged but none of the original traders remains.

The upper floors above Ladbrokes are soon to be converted back to housing to encourage more people to return to live in the city centre. This will add new life and custom to the shops and streets, more in the fashion of other European regional capitals.

Photo: Craig Oliphant

25(a) Low Friar Street / Newgate Street 1879

Photo: Newcastle Libraries

The Three Tuns Inn on the corner of Newgate Street and Low Friar Street was one of many pubs which catered for visitors to the market in this area around the White Cross (see page 44). The pub gained a bad reputation because of its unruly and immoral customers and eventually lost its licence in 1906. The building stood empty for many years until it was demolished in 1922 in order to build the tiled furniture warehouse we see there today. The Co-operative Wholesale Society took over the buildings in the 1950's for the sale of home furnishings. On the extreme right of the 1999 photograph is Newgate House, home to the much-loved Mayfair Ballroom. Both buildings are scheduled for demolition in the new millennium which has upset many residents who regard the Mayfair as part of their cultural heritage.

There is a link between photographs (a), (b), and (c).

The New Gate
Newgate Street took its name from a new gate which was constructed in the town wall in the 13th century. The gate was located at the junction of Newgate Street, Gallowgate, and Blackett Street.

25(b) 1950's

25(c) 1999

26(a) Darn Crook 1890

Darn Crook, meaning obscure or crooked street was home to Newcastle's tanning industry. The advertising billboard shows Andrews Liver Salt which was actually invented in the City. The street is now called St Andrews Street after the church to the right. In the distance are the Newcastle Breweries home of the legendary Newcastle Brown Ale.

26(b) St Andrews Street 1999

Photo: Geoff Phillips

27(a) Green Market, Newgate Street c1900

The Newgate Street Green Market was one of Newcastle's many specialised outdoor markets that stretched from the New Gate in the Town Wall, down Newgate Street, through the Bigg Market, to just past St Nicholas Church. The building on the left of the above photograph is Bourgognes public house formerly the Masons Arms. It was originally the home of the town jailor in the eighteenth century.

27(b) 1990

In 1931 the buildings on the right of the 1900 photograph were cleared for the new flagship Cooperative Stores designed by L G Ekins, CWS architect. The short section beyond the second tower was added in 1959 in replica.

Photo: Craig Oliphant

28(a) Top of Darn Crook 1890's

This picture was taken looking east towards Newgate Street. At one time Darn Crook only ran as far as the Town Wall (part of which may be seen on the left of photographs (b) and (c)) until 1810 when a new way called Heron Street was cut through to join up with Gallowgate.

The windmill was damaged by fire in the nineteenth century and was demolished in 1896.

The building you see here was erected in 1902 on the site of the old windmill. The photograph was probably taken on a match day as most of the pedestrians seem to be heading in the direction of St James' Park football ground. Some very fine motor cars enjoyed free parking in Newcastle before the parking meter era.

Photo: Jack Phillips

28(c) 1999

The street is now called St Andrews Street. Part of the Town Wall still remains, seen at the left. A multistorey car park built in the 1970's as part of the Eldon Square Shopping Centre can be seen on Newgate Street in the distance.

Photo: Geoff Phillips

This photograph shows the Kings Head pub on the corner of Percy Street and Blackett Street. On the right of the photograph is a small child who appears to be playing in the street unsupervised. It's doubtful whether a mother would allow this to happen today.

Apart from a change of brewery, and the loss of its decorative ironwork, the pub seems to have changed very little in the 1950's photograph. In the 1970's this part of the town was demolished to build the Eldon Square shopping centre as can be seen in the 1999 photograph.

The photographs on pages 62 and 63 show the scene on the opposite side of Percy Street where it meets Gallowgate. The shops to the right of centre were built in 1706. The building to the left was the premises of T Howe. The 1960 photograph shows the old shops have survived and T Howe has moved to new premises to the right. The bulldozers moved in during the 1960's despite efforts to save the historic shops. Although T Howe is no longer trading, the company's name may still be seen in fancy metal lettering above the first floor windows. The lettering still survives today; a nice reminder of past businesses.

29(b) 1950's

Photo:
Jack Phillips

29(c) 1999

Photo:
Geoff Phillips

30(a) Percy Street / Gallowgate 1895

30(b) Percy Street / Gallowgate 1960

Photo: Jack Phillips

30(c) 1966

Photo: Jack Phillips

30(d) 1999

Photo: Geoff Phillips

31(a) Percy Street / Gallowgate 2   1895

31(b)   1999

Photo: Geoff Phillips

32(a) Percy Street / Leazes Lane 1910

The Morpeth Castle pub, noted for its Bass ales, stood on the corner of Leazes Lane and Percy Street. The pub did not have a cellar and beer was drawn from barrels mounted on a gantry in the bar.

The building was home to Ainsleys Fireplace shop in the 1960's but is now occupied by Durham Pine furniture shop.

32(b)   1990's

Photo: Craig Oliphant

33(a) Percy Street 1880

This remarkable picture shows Percy Street in 1880. The building at the top left is the Jewish Synagogue on Leazes Park Road.

The 1960's photograph shows Handyside Arcade on the far right which was renamed Arcadia during the 'Swinging Sixties'. There were dozens of small boutiques selling the latest fashions and 'flower power' paraphernalia. There were several musical instrument stores and sound amplification manufacturers to cater for the Geordie Scene. The building housed the legendary Club a Go Go where the famous Newcastle band 'The Animals' played, also on the extreme right is Jeavons music store; the company also had stores in Pudding Chare and Wallsend.

The Jewish Synagogue became Leazes Arcade which was badly damaged by fire in the early 1990's. The remaining shell was later refurbished to provide student accommodation. The ground floor is a comedy club called Hyena Cafe. The new buildings in the centre of the 1999 photograph form part of Eldon Gardens, a later extension to the Eldon Square shopping complex.

33(b) Percy Street 1960's

Photo: Jack Phillips

33(c) 1999

Photo: Geoff Phillips

34(a) Farmers' Rest, Haymarket 1890

34(b) Farmers' Rest, Haymarket 1920

34(c) Farmers' Rest, Haymarket 1990

Photograph (a) on the opposite page shows the very first Farmers' Rest pub in 1890. By 1920 a smart new pub had been built with Newcastle Breweries Ginger Beer Works behind.

The pub met its demise in 1995 when Marks and Spencer extended its store through to the Haymarket: the company's marketing buzz word for the new store was 'M&SSIVE'.

This area also boasts a brand new covered bus station with soothing music playing over loudspeakers.

Photo: Craig Oliphant

34(d) Marks and Spencer and New Bus Station 1999

Photo: Geoff Phillips

The Haymarket was first used in 1824 as an area in the town centre where farmers would bring hay and straw to be sold. At one time it was also known as Parade Ground as the Newcastle Volunteers would assemble here for inspection. Public meetings were often held in the Haymarket and, in particular, the temperance reformer Dr Rutherford would preach about the evils of drink. A memorial to Dr Rutherford may be seen in Bigg Market. (See page 48.)

Newcastle historian, R J Charleton wrote about the Haymarket in 1893:
Here come the wild beast shows which visit Newcastle, together with the attendant exhibitions of waxworks, fat ladies, and living skeletons.

St Thomas Church, designed by John Dobson, was erected in 1830 on the site of St Mary Magdalene leper hospital. The church was built to replace St Thomas Chapel which was situated at the north end of the old stone Tyne Bridge until 1828. On the extreme left of the photograph is the Grand Hotel built in 1890 by James Deuchar.

The 1975 photograph shows the well-known bronze statue of an angel which was erected in 1908 in memory of the soldiers who died in the Boer War. Soon after the 1975 photograph was taken, the bronze angel was temporarily removed and placed in storage in case it was damaged by vibration from the drilling for the Metro underground. To the right of the church is the tower of Newcastle's Civic Centre completed in 1967.

The 1999 photograph shows the distinctive circular design of the Haymarket Metro station.

35(b) 1975

Photo: Jack Phillips

35(c) 1999

Photo: Geoff Phillips

36(a) Percy Street

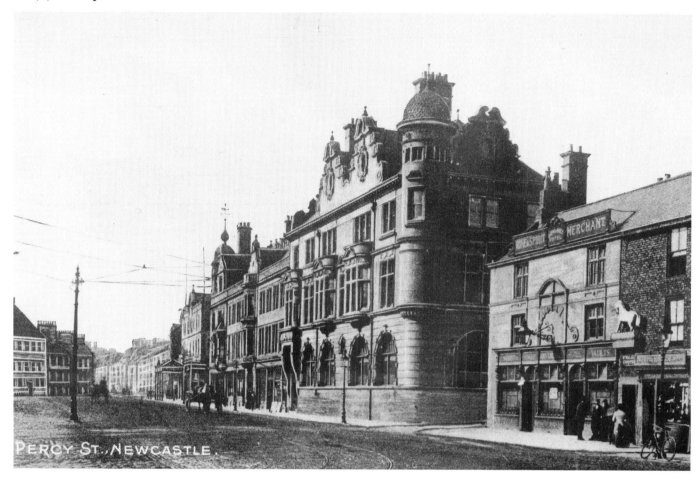

The large building in the centre of the photograph is the former Newcastle Breweries offices. Designed by Joseph Oswald, architect, and built between 1896 and 1900, it contains a very richly decorated interior of ornamental tiling, mahogany panelling, carved mahogany chimney pieces, and marble staircases with wrought iron balustrades. The building is now used by Newcastle University. The building to the right is the Haymarket Hotel public house. It is believed that the pub was originally the eighteenth century home of a policeman called Nixon. The house was converted into a pub in 1833. In the late 1980's the pub was earmarked for demolition. A group of Newcastle University students along with locals tried in vain to prevent its demolition but 1987 saw its demise for the sake of extra car parking spaces for the University.

To the left of the Newcastle Breweries building can be seen the decorative canopy that marks the entrance to the old Palace Theatre. Built in 1879 as a general purpose hall for circus performances and Sunday lectures, in 1890 it became the People's Palace of Variety. From 1895 until its demolition in the early 1960's, it was simply called the Palace Theatre and provided a mixed programme of drama and pantomime.

36(b) 1966

Photo: Jack Phillips

36(c) 1999

Photo: Geoff Phillips

37(a) Barras Bridge 1906

KINGS VISIT.
BARRASS BRIDGE NEWCASTLE. JULY.11.1906. G.H.N/c.
5192.

This photograph shows Mr Phillips' (no relation) food store on Barras Bridge on 11 July 1906, the date of the visit to Newcastle upon Tyne by King Edward VII.

There are two schools of thought as to the derivation of the name Barras. Some historians think it may be a corruption of the word 'barriers'. The other explanation is that Barras is a corruption of barrows being a medieval word for a burial mound. There would have been many people buried at this spot in ancient times as there was a leprosy hospital where St Thomas Church now stands.

There was certainly a bridge at Barras Bridge which spanned Pandon Dene, a tributary of the River Tyne which ran through this spot. The sketch opposite shows the bridge c1800.

The 1950's photograph shows me posing rather reluctantly for the photographer. The Phillips' business has moved to the premises on the right.

The 1999 photograph is taken from the same spot and shows the Newcastle Playhouse. The area is now part of the University of Newcastle upon Tyne.

37(b) Barras Bridge 1950's

Photo: Jack Phillips

37(c) Newcastle Playhouse 1999

Photo: Geoff Phillips

38(a) Northumberland Road c1910

The White City building of 1893 in the centre was once a skating rink. It was replaced on this site by the Hippodrome theatre in 1912. This theatre closed in 1933.

The original Olympia was built in 1893 and was destroyed by fire in 1907. The Olympia cinema shown in the photograph above was built in 1909 and closed for business in 1961.

The Tudor style building which may be seen on the left of the 1999 photograph was originally home to Tilley's restaurant. In 1971 Scottish and Newcastle Breweries converted it to a trendy new pub called the City Tavern where you could drink Youngers' Tartan beer and eat beef with cider and orange. The building is now home to Huxters Sports Bar.

In the late 1990's the north end of Northumberland Street was pedestrianised so there is no longer vehicle access from Northumberland Road. The steel canopy jutting out above the cars on the left is the entrance to the Pacific Bar, a magnificent new building constructed from steel, granite and glass.

**White City Skating Rink
Northumberland Road**

38(b) Northumberland Road 1966

Photo: Jack Phillips

38(c) 1999

Photo: Geoff Phillips

39(a) Fenwick's Store, Northumberland Street 1900's

39(b) 1999

It was 1882 when John James Fenwick, a Newcastle draper, opened his first store at No5 Northumberland Street. A year later he moved to No39 Northumberland Street which was vacant. No39 was one of a pair of stone houses which were built in 1820 for a Newcastle doctor. The next year Mr Fenwick acquired the second house and the photograph above shows the frontage of his shop in the early 1900's.

Further expansion of the Northumberland Street frontage was hindered by the fact that the owner of the Oak Leaf pub next door would not sell. Not to be frustrated, John Fenwick opened a fur store on the other side of the street and then opened a store in Bond Street London. He sent his eldest sons, Fred and Arthur to Paris to learn the fashion business.

The company took a major step forward when they purchased the Burnup coach building factory which stretched from behind the store to Eldon Square. A large retail hall was built on the land and the business changed from an exclusive tailoring establishment to a department store.

Photo: Geoff Phillips

40(a) Fenwick's Terrace Tea Rooms 1950's

Photo:
Fenwick Collection

The owner of the Oak Leaf eventually agreed to sell and a brand new frontage for the store in white Carrara ware was completed in 1913. Over the last 30 years a 'master plan' for the rebuilding of the store has been implemented resulting in the present day building which has six floors and a magnificent 150 foot Northumberland Street frontage.

40(b) Fenwick's Terrace Restaurant 1999

Photo: Geoff Phillips

41(a) Northumberland Street (north) 1920

The above photograph shows some of the businesses
at the north end of Northumberland Street.

41(b) 1990's

Photo:
Craig Oliphant

42(a) Northumberland Street c1905

Photo: The Fenwick Collection

On the right is Jackson House which housed the Star Hotel. Fenwick's store may just be seen above the man with the bowler hat in the centre of the photograph.

42(b) Northumberland Street 1999

Photo: Geoff Phillips

43(a) Northumberland Street 1897

This is one of my favourite photographs and shows Northumberland Street at the time of Queen Victoria's Diamond Jubilee. The policeman in the centre of the photograph gives a reassurance that everything is under control.

The street is decorated with bunting once more in the 1937 photograph; this time to celebrate the coronation of George VI. This photograph shows how inadequate the pavements were on this busy shopping street, but it was another 40 years before the street was pedestrianised. There is an interesting link between all three photographs.

The four photographs on pages 84 and 85 show the corner of Blackett Street and Northumberland Street. At first sight it would seem that the 1896 photograph was taken on a quiet Sunday morning. Closer inspection reveals a ghostly blur along the pavements which indicates that the photograph was taken using a long exposure time so that the walking pedestrians may not be seen. The street was probably as busy as in the other three photographs.

The 1938 photograph was taken from the balcony of the Paramount cinema (now the Odeon) and shows how busy this street used to be. Notice that trams, trolley buses and motor buses were in service simultaneously.

In 1953 there was still complete chaos at this junction as Northumberland Street had to carry the main north-south A1 trunk-road traffic as well as local traffic. Cook's corner, which took its name from the travel agent located there, may be seen on the right . The pavements are filled to capacity; the pedestrians having to pick their way carefully through the traffic at the junction. A pedestrian bridge stood here for a short time in the 1960's to help the situation.

In the centre of the 1999 photograph is Monument Mall completed in 1992. Northumberland Street was given over totally to pedestrians in 1998. On the left is the Northern Goldsmith's building which underwent refurbishment in 1999, including a novel external lighting scheme.

43(b) Northumberland Street 1937

43(c) 1999

Photo: Geoff Phillips

44(a) Northumberland Street / Blackett Street   1896

44(b)   1938

45(a) Blackett Street c1900

Blackett Street was built in 1824 and followed the line of the north section of the old town wall. The 1999 photograph shows Monument Mall on the left where the original facades of some of the earlier buildings were retained and incorporated in the new design.

45(b) 1999

Photo: Geoff Phillips

46(a) Emerson Chambers, Blackett Street c1905

46(b) Emerson Chambers, Blackett Street 1999

47(a) Grey's Monument 1930

Built in 1838 to commemorate the great work carried out by Charles, Earl Grey on the Reform Bill of 1832, the "Roman Doric Column" stands over 130 ft. high and the statue of Earl Grey faces down the street named after him. The monument was designed by John and Benjamin Green who also designed Penshaw Monument.

The elegant building on the left housed the YMCA and had to give way to the Eldon Square shopping centre. Some of the stone carvings from this building were saved and incorporated into the brickwork of the Northumberland Arms pub which is just off Northumberland Street near to the entrance of Eldon Square shopping centre.

47(b) Grey's Monument 1966

Photo: Jack Phillips

47(c) Grey's Monument 1999

The old, flat-roofed post office building shown in the photograph above was demolished in order to build Monument Mall which is a splendid piece of Pastiche architecture similar in style to buildings erected by Grainger over 100 years ago. This area has now been re-paved with Caithness stone slabs.

Photo: Geoff Phillips

New Bridge Street was constructed in 1812 and was intended as an alternative route to North Shields. It took its name from a bridge which was built over Pandon Burn which was a tributary of the River Tyne. The new bridge must have been roughly where the Central Motorway East passes under the roundabout near to the Warner Brothers Cinema complex.

The church in the centre with the two spires is the Trinity Presbyterian Church and to its right is the Church of the Divine Unity. Both Churches were designed by John Dobson, one of Newcastle's finest architects, who lived on this street for a while.   The building on the far right is the Newcastle upon Tyne Free Library. When the Free Library Act was adopted by Newcastle upon Tyne, it was decided to build a library on the site of Carliol Tower which was part of the Town Wall. There were many objections to this plan resulting in protest meetings and petitions, but to no avail. On 21 May 1880 the tower was demolished and construction of the Free Library commenced. The library was opened on 7 December 1881.

The building on the left may be the original Burton House pub on Croft Street. The Burton House shown on the 1987 photograph was built in 1931 but went for a Burton in 1989 to clear the way for the extension to John Dobson Street and Portland Buildings, home to the Newcastle Building Society.

Newcastle's new Central Library with the distinctive concrete flutes was completed in 1968 and is shown in the two later photographs. John Dobson Street built in 1970 is seen to emerge from underneath the concrete deck to the east of the library. The deck was part of an elevated network of pedestrian routes which was the beginning of a futuristic plan to vertically separate road traffic from pedestrian traffic in Newcastle - a plan which did not come to fruition. Most of the concrete deck was removed in the 1990's and John Dobson Street was extended south to Market Street.

A smart new frontage has been built for the Laing Art Gallery seen on the right of the 1999 photograph and trees have been planted on this part of New Bridge Street which is no longer a through-route.

48(b) 1987

Photo: Craig Oliphant

48(c) 1999

49(a) Pilgrim Street c1912

The large white building in the centre of the 1912 photograph is Northern Counties Conservative Club built in 1911. The Paramount cinema, now called the Odeon is yet to be built. The line of Pilgrim Street is now ruined by the Commercial Union office block which straddles the southbound carriageway. How on earth was planning permission given for such a monstrosity?

**49(b)
1999**

*Photo:
Geoff Phillips*

50(a) Market Street 1905

Market Street was built in 1840 connecting Grainger Street with Pilgrim Street. The building on the right is the Central Exchange which was originally built between 1836 and 1838, and rebuilt internally in 1905 after a fire. The design was based on the Temple of Vesta at Tivoli and was originally planned as a commodity exchange. It now houses the magnificent Central Arcade with its beautiful faience tile work.

50(b) 1999

Photo: Geoff Phillips

51(a) Market Street / Pilgrim Street c1900

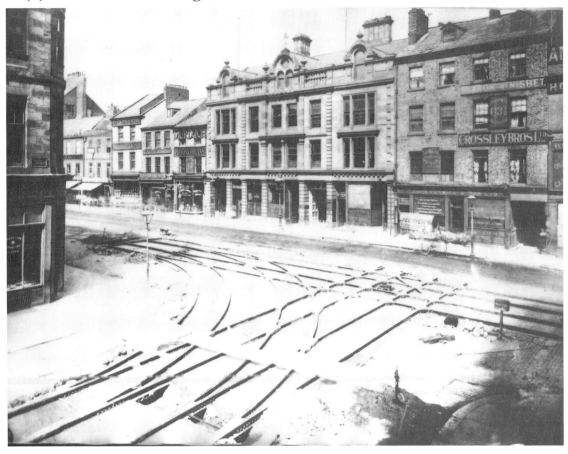

When Market Street was built in 1840 it only ran as far as Pilgrim Street. The view above shows this but as the tram lines are being laid provision is made for the Market Street extension, completed in 1906.

51(b) 1999

Carliol House, built for the North-East Electricity Supply Company, has graced this corner of Market Street since 1927. The building is faced in white Portland stone, the stone of London's St Pauls Cathedral. It was very fashionable between the wars for adding a monumentability to new office buildings.

Photo: Geoff Phillips

52(a) Pilgrim Street /
Mosley Street 1900

This remarkable photograph shows the corner of Mosley Street and Pilgrim Street when extensive road excavations were underway.

In the centre of the photograph is the Friends Meeting House which bears the date 1698 above the door. My father's notes record that the Quaker movement held their first service in their meeting house on Pilgrim Street in 1688. Meetings were held there for 273 years until the City bought the properties along this part of the street to build the Pilgrim Street roundabout in the early 1960's. Another famous building which met its demise at the time was Grainger's Royal Arcade built in 1832 and seen on the right of the photograph. The Royal Arcade was designed to be a fashionable mall of the day with offices, shops and banks. It was built too far away from the centre of the City, however, and

the tenants gradually moved out. In 1966 the stonework was carefully dismantled and each stone was numbered with the intention of rebuilding the Arcade elsewhere. It never happened and as a compromise, a facsimile of the interior of the Arcade was built in wood and plaster on the ground floor of Swan House, the office block seen on the right of the 1999 photograph.

I would like to thank Mr Harrison of Short, Richardson, and Forth for allowing me to take the 1999 photograph from the window of their premises.

52(b) Pilgrim Street /
Mosley Street 1999

Photo: Geoff Phillips

In the middle ages, pilgrimages were fashionable among the more religious and well-off English folk. Pilgrims travelling from the south to visit the Chapel of the Blessed Mary at Jesmond would enter Newcastle through a gate in the town wall which became known as Pilgrims' Gate. Weary from their journey, many Pilgrims would find lodgings in the many inns on the street near to Pilgrims' Gate and the street became known as Pilgrim Street.

The photograph above was taken in 1920 before the Tyne Bridge was built. Pilgrim Street continues through the railway arch and may be seen curving left and descending towards All Saints Church. The shop on the left is G Cook's fish and chip salon and next to that is the barber: C E Pearson. The projecting sign outside his shop enquires: 'Shave Sir?'

The 1950's photograph was taken from the same spot and shows the approach to the Tyne Bridge. All Saints Church was built between 1786 and 1796 but records show there was a church on this site before the end of the 12th century.

The 1999 photograph shows the enormous changes which have taken place in the last 40 years. In the late 1960's a roundabout was built at this site to relieve the traffic congestion. In the 1970's a through-traffic underpass was built as part of the Central Motorway East along with a labyrinth of pedestrian walkways and tunnels.

53(b) Pilgrim Street 1950's

Photo: Jack Phillips

53(c) 1999

Photo: Geoff Phillips

54(a) Low Pilgrim Street c1925

Before the Tyne Bridge was built in 1928 Pilgrim Street used to continue downhill and was one of the main routes to the Quayside. Pilgrim Street passed All Saints Church which is to the right, out of camera shot in photograph (a). On reaching this spot travellers could turn right and continue down Akenside Hill to the Quayside. An alternative route would be down Dog Bank to Broad Chare.

R J Charleton, author of 'A History of Newcastle-on-Tyne' in 1893, describes this part of town:

'Pilgrim Street below the Arcade presents a decidedly forlorn appearance. Frowsy public houses, small provision shops, furniture brokers, and marine store dealers, are all plentiful. On either side narrow passages and courts lead to pent-up crowded masses of dwellings, if we may so term these abodes of poverty and misery. Common lodging houses, where tramps and cadgers sojourn, are numerous in these dark recesses, as testified by their sign-boards, announcing the incredible number of travellers they are licensed to entertain. Poverty and idleness, it can be plainly seen, are old inhabitants of Low Pilgrim Street, nor can it be said that vice and crime are strangers to its air. Groups of men are generally seen standing about, hands deep in pockets, knocking their heels together, smoking and talking in that strange manner peculiar to their class, without in the least looking at one another as people generally do in conversation, but gazing straight forward over the way at something else. Women, bedraggled, and generally carrying children in their arms, or with children hanging on by their skirts, also gather in groups and gossip together, disappearing at intervals into the public houses.'

54(b) 1960's

This photograph shows the same scene in the 1960's and this part of Pilgrim Street is now run down and forgotten. The tower of St Nicholas Cathedral may be seen poking above the approach road to the Tyne Bridge.

The busy shops with housing above on the approach to the old steps, have now been reduced to unused ground floor facades only

Photo: Jack Phillips

54(c) 1999

The scene is now dominated by the All Saints office block.

The stairs in the foreground were refurbished by the Tyne and Wear Council in the late 1970's by referring to early photographs like the one shown on the opposite page.

Photo: Geoff Phillips

Dog Bank was a narrow street which ran from Low Pilgrim Street to Broad Chare in Pandon. It passed through part of the most densely populated area of nineteenth century Newcastle. The house in the centre of the picture is typical of the period and shows ascending storeys jutting out further and further above the street thereby giving more living space on the upper floors. On some of the narrowest chares residents of the top floor could sometimes be close enough to shake hands with their neighbour across the street. The pub on the left may be the Marquis of Granby which was often frequented by parishioners of All Saints Church.

55(b) Dog Bank   1987

This is the same view down Dog Bank in 1987 when contractors were commencing construction of the new housing seen in the 1999 photograph.

Only one side of Dog Bank has been developed so that the residents could enjoy sunny views over Newcastle's splendid Quayside.

Photo: Craig Oliphant

55(c) Dog Bank   1999

Photo: Geoff Phillips

This is another view of Dog Bank looking uphill towards Low Pilgrim Street. The same tiered houses with projecting lamp brackets can be seen in the centre of the photograph. Although this is in the centre of a growing city, the chicken pecking its way along the cobbles would have been a familiar sight. The existence of the grand doorcase on the right, and the handsome bow windows of the shop on the left, suggests that this area may have had a more elegant and affluent past.

There is no link between photograph (a) and (b) unless you want to count the cobble stones!

56(b) Dog Bank   1989

Photo: Craig Oliphant

56(c) Dog Bank   1999

Photo: Geoff Phillips

At the foot of Dog Bank was the area of the town known as Pandon. In the late 1800's it had the worst slums in the City with one of the highest death rates in England. Pandon Burn, a tributary of the River Tyne passed through this area bringing with it pollution from parts of the town further upstream. Outbreaks of cholera, typhus and smallpox took their toll on the population of this grim part of town.

The photograph above shows the street called Cowgate leading to Broad Chare which is behind the man reading the paper. To the left is Blyth Nook which was a narrow lane leading to the street called Pandon.

57(b) Cowgate / Broad Chare 1950's

My father took this photograph in the 1950's and it shows the area to be in need of renovation following selective demolition. To the right is Dog Bank which was shown in the previous photographs.

The area which was known as Pandon is now occupied by an enormous car park for the new Law Courts. The building next to the white van in the photograph below is Trinity House, on Broad Chare which has been home to the Master Mariners of Newcastle since 1505 although the buildings seen here are mostly of 18th century origin.

Photo: Jack Phillips

57(c) 1999

Photo: Geoff Phillips

Photo: Newcastle Libraries

The view above shows the corner of Milk Market and Sandgate looking east. At the time the photograph was taken there were over two dozen pubs on this street to cater for the thirsts of countless seamen who would frequent this part of town. In the seventeenth and eighteenth centuries this area was home to Newcastle's Keelmen who navigated the flat bottomed vessels called keels which were used to transport coal from staiths to large ships waiting in deeper water.

The Three Bulls Heads pub on the right advertises 'good beds' which would be a luxury for seafarers used to poor ship-board accommodation. The structure on the left is a pant which was a public drinking water fountain. The pub to the left of the pant is probably the Grey Horse Inn.

The 1950's photograph shows the area to be forgotten and neglected. The only pub remaining was probably the Lord Nelson which is the second building along on the left.

In the 1990's a breathtaking transformation took place bringing Sandgate into the 21st century. The seedy pubs have been replaced by up-market themed restaurants and bars and the Co-operative warehouse seen on the right of the 1950 photograph has been converted into the Malmaison Hotel.

58(b) Sandgate c1950

Photo: Geoff Phillips

58(c) Sandgate 1999

59(a) Gilroy's Spirit Vaults, Quayside 1890

Gilroy's Spirit Vaults was a public House located at 134 Quayside. Right next door are the very old premises of W F Scott - Ship Lamp Maker and Tin Plate Worker.

The 1950's photograph shows my father Jack Phillips sitting on the step of what is left of W F Scott's workshop. The pub remains, however, and trades as the New Sun Inn; a Fitzgerald house. Thomas Hedley's soap works may be seen behind the pub.

Spot the deliberate mistake.

59(b) 1950

Photo: Jack Phillips

59(c) 1999

Photo: Geoff Phillips

This area had previously been devastated by the great fire of 1854 caused by an explosion in a warehouse across the river in Gateshead.

At the time this photograph was taken there were only two bridges across the Tyne at this point: the Swing Bridge and the High Level Bridge.

There were many pubs on the Quayside; the one on the right of the photograph is the Scotch Arms, further down, at No10 was the Bridge Inn and next to that was the Turks Head. The distinctive lamp which juts out from the side of the building at the end belonged to the Ship public house.

There were many narrow lanes called Chares which ran from the Quayside to Butcher Bank (now called Akenside Hill), Dog Bank or Pandon. The lane on the right of the photograph above is Cocks Chare named after Alderman Cock who lived there at one time. Some maps show the spelling to be Cox Chare and my father's notes record that the street signs at each end

60(b) Quayside 1999

Photo: Geoff Phillips

of this Chare had the two different spellings. The next lane, which was between the Turks Head and the Bridge Inn, was Byker Chare which is thought to have been named after Robert de Byker who owned premises in Pandon. The next lane was Burn Bank so named because it followed the course of Pandon Burn.

Spicer Lane came next and then Broad Chare which still remains today.

The 1999 photograph shows this area to be occupied by the new law courts completed in 1990.

61(a) Ouseburn Vale, Byker 1964

Photo: Newcastle Libraries

The Ouseburn is a tributary of the River Tyne. The photograph above shows the burn flowing through a part of Byker which is badly in need of improvement.

In the early 1970's a breathtaking transformation took place. The rubbish was cleared and the vale landscaped. The vale is now home to City Farm Byker.

61(b) 1999

Photo: Geoff Phillips

62(a) Shields Road, Byker c1910

At the turn of the nineteenth century Shields Road was a busy shopping thoroughfare; this is a view looking east. A bypass to the south now takes through traffic away from this part of Shields Road.

62(b) 1999

*Photo:
Geoff Phillips*

C.A. PARSONS & Co Ltd SHIELDS RD N/c
1900

Sir Charles Algernon Parsons was given the informal title 'The man who invented the twentieth century'. He invented the steam turbine when working as a junior partner of Clarke Chapman. He started his steam turbine manufacturing business on Shields Road in 1889 when the works occupied a site of 2 acres with a staff of 48.

Parsons' turbines were far superior to the conventional reciprocating steam engines. The first ship to be fitted with a Parsons' steam turbine was the Turbinia which achieved speeds of 34.5 knots during its naval trials in the Solent in 1897. Such speeds had never been recorded before and the Admiralty were impressed enough to order two ships, Cobra and Viper, to be powered by Parsons' turbines.

Parsons' turbines were soon fitted as standard in ships built in the Tyne's shipyards, the most famous ship being the Mauretania, launched at Wallsend in 1906 and described as 'The floating palace'.
Steam turbines were also adopted by the electricity generating industry and orders were coming in from countries throughout the world. By the time of the 1950 photograph on the opposite page, the size of the works had increased multifold and turbines capable of generating 100MW of power were in production. On the extreme right of the 1950 picture is '0' bay which was completed in 1948 to facilitate the construction of the much larger turbines.

In 1951 construction of a new research and development building commenced which was to occupy the site of Parsons original factory. The futuristic, six storey building was completed in 1953 and incorporated some novel features for its day, such as double glazing, cold cathode strip lighting, heating by low pressure hot water which circulated in pipes situated behind the ceiling lighting reflectors, ventilation, sound-proofing, and Paternoster continuous lifts. The lift cubicles were connected in a chain link fashion and ran continuously in a vertical loop. There weren't any doors, you just waited until a vacant cubicle arrived and jumped on while it was moving. As a Parsons apprentice in the 1960's I remember being fooled into thinking that the lift cubicles turned upside down when they reached the top of the building. Older colleagues would delight in forcing you to ride a Paternoster through the loft and watch your face go green as you thought it was going to turn 180 degrees.

In the 1990's Parsons was bought out by the German company Siemens.

63(b) 1950

63(c) Siemens Power Generation Ltd 1999

64(a) Wolsington Hotel, Walkergate 1905

Further east along Shields Road is Walkergate and two very old pubs: the Wolsington Hotel (which used to be nicknamed 'Seaman Watsons' after the ex-boxer former manager) and the Colliery Engine Inn. Both pubs survive today as can be seen in the photograph below.

64(b)   1999

Photo: Geoff Phillips

65(a) Armstrong Bridge, Jesmond c1900

'Sir William's Bridge', as the locals called it, was designed by Tyneside's famous industrialist, William George Armstong and was completed in 1878. It provided a welcome alternative route to Benton Bank which was a steep climb for a horse and cart. Motor vehicles started to use the bridge and this must have contributed to its deterioration. In 1963 it was closed to road traffic and the City Council considered demolishing it due to the enormous renovation costs. The bridge survives today for pedestrian use only, and is the venue for a craft fair on Sundays.

65(b) Armstrong Bridge, Jesmond 1999

Photo: Geoff Phillips

66(a) Blue Bell pub, Jesmond Vale 1914

Further upstream of the Ouseburn is the beautiful Jesmond Vale. The photograph above shows St Christopher's Mission on the left and the Blue Bell pub on the right.

R J Charleton, author of 'A History of Newcastle-on-Tyne', visited this part of Newcastle in 1893 and described what he saw:

We left the Ouseburn at Heaton Haugh, and here again we join it to wander further up its valley. No longer bordered by crowding houses and factories, no longer gliding under a cloud of smoke and choked with slimy impurities, but flowing between grassy banks and overhung by waving trees we see the burn. Rather trodden and broken down, it is true, are its banks here about, but not the less beautiful when we consider that its condition is the evidence of its usefulness. Lovely, indeed, is the undisturbed beauty of the country when, far from the madding crowd, it is seen and enjoyed by the few; but there is something beyond loveliness - something gladdening though touching - in the sight of nature, trampled and worn, yet still beautiful, offering itself a sacrifice, and a sacrifice not in vain, for the good of the many. Every downtrodden blade of grass, every foot-worn stone by the edge of the stream, every naked wound in the galled withers of the earth, is full of beauty when we consider the happy crowds which have caused the ruin, and the happy hours which have been passed in unintentionally accomplishing it. "Up the Burn!" What memories of boyhood's days, what visions of surpassing and long passed enjoyment, do these words recall to thousands of Newcastle people now toiling in the town of their birth or in other parts of the world! What hopes do they not excite in thousands of young hearts still, yearning for Saturday morning and the long day by the burnside!

In view (b) the Sinfonia Centre, built in the late 1960's, may just be seen through the trees on the left. View (c) shows the Blue Bell pub is still in business.

66(b) 1990

Photo: Craig Oliphant

66(c) 1999

Photo: Geoff Phillips

67(a) Jesmond Road c1920

Heavy rainfall has caused severe flooding in Jesmond Road at the junction with Shortridge Terrace. Local residents stare in amazement as the waves lap against Mr Elliot's store.

View (b) was taken fifty years later and shows my father Jack Phillips surveying the same location. The store is now a bank.

A map dated 1898 shows a house called Wellburn in its own grounds which occupied the area on the right of the above photograph. Wellburn was the first private house in Newcastle to be fitted out with electric lighting. The area to the north of where the photograph was taken is now known as Wellburn Park.

View (c) shows there to be little change in the architecture, but the building of the Coast Road extension means that through traffic is now diverted from this part of Jesmond.

67(b) Jesmond Road c1970

67(c) 1999

Photo:
June Phillips

68(a) West Road / Slatyford Lane, Denton Burn c1900

**68(b)
1940's**

**68(c)
1999**

*Photo:
Geoff Phillips*

69(a) Fox and Hounds pub, West Road c1898

The three photographs on the opposite page show the West Road where it intersects with Slatyford Lane. The West Road or West Turnpike as it was known, follows the course of the Roman Wall.   Further east, towards Newcastle, was the original Fox and Hounds pub built in about 1898. This is shown in the photograph above. Two Ball Lonnen is the road seen leading off to the left after the street lamp. On the right are the grounds of West Acres owned by Benjamin Browne, Chairman of Hawthorn Leslie.

69(b) New Fox and Hounds pub, West Road 1999

Photo: Geoff Phillips

70(a) Benwell Village

Benwell is an area of Newcastle which is steeped in history. It is said that coal was first mined here by the Romans. In medieval times this area was owned by the very powerful Delaval family after which it was taken over by the Shaftoes (of Bobby Shaftoe fame). The building behind the trees is Benwell Tower, designed by Dobson, and completed in 1831. It became home to the newly appointed Bishop of Newcastle in 1881, the year before Newcastle attained the status of a city. More recently, Benwell Tower was used as a location for the popular children's television programme 'Byker Grove'.

70(b)
1999

Photo:
Geoff Phillips

The Links Between the Old and New Photographs

If the links are obvious, they are not included in this list.

1. Tyne Bridge
The most obvious link is the bridge but notice that in the modern photograph there is a lamp at the end of the wall which is a replica of the lamp in the old photograph.

2. Side
Notice that the bracket for the Spirit Vaults lamp on the left of shot (a) may still be seen in shot (b).

4. Castle Garth
Notice the Black Gate to the left of the cathedral is the same.

6. Westgate Road / Collingwood Street
The link between shots (a) and (c) is the building in the distance, but notice that shot (b) shows that extra floors have been added to the building on the extreme right on shot (a).

7. Bewick Street
The obvious link is Bewick House on the left but notice the gable end of the old post office on Pink Lane may be seen poking above Gunner House above the 'Welcome' sign.

8. Scotswood Road
Obviously the buildings on the left are the same, and St Mary's Church spire and the Market Keeper's house remain.

9. Blenheim Street /Scotswood Road
The link is Rockie's Bar on the extreme right of the 1999 picture.

10. Sunderland Street / Blenheim Street
The spires of Blandford House (Discovery Museum) are the links.

11. Westgate Road / Lockhart's Cocoa Rooms
The links between all three photographs are the buildings at the extreme right and left.

12. Clayton Street / Pink Lane
The link between all three shots is the small building in the distance on the left, also the gable end above it.

13. Clayton Street / Westgate Road
Most of the buildings remain the same except the cinema but notice extra stonework has been added to the building in the centre.

14. Westgate Road
The dome of the building on the left of shot (a) may be seen in shot (b).

16. Fenkle Street
The link is the building above the 'Riman and Co Ltd' sign.

17. Blackfriars
Notice on shot (a) that the stone window arches have been bricked up, but have been restored to their former glory in shot (c). My father placed me in the wrong spot for photograph (b). To be in the same spot as the woman in shot (a), I should have stood further to the right where you see the shadow of a gable end.

18. Newgate Street / White Cross
The link between (a) and (c) is the IBM building on the far left.

19. Bigg Market
The curved stonework at the top left is one of the links between (a) and (b). The two buildings to the right of the Half Moon pub in (b) may be seen in (a). The building with the curved attic windows in the centre of the photograph is the same in (a), (b), and (c).

20. Corn Exchange & Old Town Hall, Bigg Market
The gable end of the building at the far left of shots (a) and (c) is the same. The two buildings below the cathedral are the same in all three photographs.

21. Bigg Market / High Bridge
The roof of the building to the left of the 'Supplied by Swinburne' sign may be the same in (b).

22. Newgate Street / Clayton Street
The obvious link is the Rose and Crown pub. Grainger's buildings on the right remain the same.

25. Low Friar Street / Newgate Street
The link between all three photographs is the gable end seen at the extreme right in shot (a).

26. Darn Crook
The link is the wall of the church on the right.

27. Green Market, Newgate Street
The links are the two gate posts of St Andrew's Church wall which may be seen above the head of the trader on the right in photograph (a).

28. Top of Darn Crook
The link between (a) and (b) is the brick wall with a door seen on the extreme left of (a).

29. Percy Street / Blackett Street
There is no link between (b) and (c).

30. Percy Street / Gallowgate
The links between (a) and (b) are the old shops. The link between (b), (c), and (d) is the T Howe building at the extreme right.

31. Percy Street / Gallowgate 2
There is no link here.

32. Percy Street / Leazes Lane
The pub and the shop are the same building. Notice how the wall on the right slopes outwards.

33. Percy Street
The link between all three photographs is the Synagogue at the top left of (a) which became Leazes Arcade, and after a fire it was re-furbished and is now student housing.

34. Farmer's Rest, Haymarket
The link between (a) and (b) is the building at the extreme right. The link between (c) and (d) is Marks and Spencer's tall building at the top right.

35. Haymarket
The link between all three photographs is the Grand Hotel building at the extreme left (now Blackwells Bookshop).

37. Barras Bridge
The link between (a) and (b) is the shop on the right. There is no link between (b) and (c).

38. Northumberland Road
The obvious link between (a) and (b) is the Olympia but notice the castellated building in the centre appears in all three photographs.

41. Northumberland Street (north)
Although the windows have been renewed, the 1920 buildings exist today. The ornate cornice is the link.

42. Northumberland Street
The link is obviously Jackson House on the right but notice the stone door-arch is still there in the 1999 photograph although the arch now has a steel frame.

43. Northumberland Street
The link between all three photographs is Amos Atkinson's shop.

44. Northumberland Street / Blackett Street
The obvious link between (a) and (b) is the corner building. Notice the ornate awning of the cinema is the same in (b) and (c). The Northern Goldsmith's building on the left remains the same in all four photographs, however, only the edge of the famous gold clock may be seen in (b).

45. Blackett Street
The obvious link is Eldon Building on the right, however, the facades of some of the buildings on the left of shot (a) have been incorporated in Monument Mall.

46. Emerson Chambers
The Chambers building is the obvious link but also part of the original Eldon Square above the young girl in the old photograph still remains today.

48. New Bridge Street
There is no link between (a) and (b).

49. Pilgrim Street
The link is the dome of the Northern Goldsmith building seen just below the lamp on the left of shot (a). Also the Grainger Town building on the corner of Pilgrim Street and Hood Street on the left. Jackson House above the double-decker bus in the 1999 photograph is also present in the 1912 photograph although it is difficult to see clearly.

51. Market Street / Pilgrim Street
The link is the Northern Rock building on the left.

52. Pilgrim Street / Mosley Street
The link is the Norwich Union building on the left.

53. Pilgrim Street
The link between (a) and (b) is the bay window of the building on the right. All Saints church is the link between (b) and (c).

54. Low Pilgrim Street
The links between all three photographs are the railings on the left and the church wall on the right.

55. Dog Bank
Notice the distinctive curve in the kerb at the bottom right of (a) and (b) is the same. There is no link in Dog Bank 2.

57. Cowgate / Broad Chare
I cannot find a link between (a) and (b), but the links between (b) and (c) are obviously the buildings in the centre of the photographs.

58. Sandgate
The houses in the distance are the same in (a) and (b) but the link between (b) and (c) is the Cooperative Warehouse on the right.

59. Gilroy's Spirit Vaults, Quayside
Although I would like to believe it, the building on the left of (b) and (c) is not the same. The building on the left of photograph (a) is the Swirl warehouse, not the Cooperative warehouse. The Swirl warehouse used to be further west from the Coop.

61. Ouseburn
Notice the bridge at the bottom left is the same. This is Crawford's Bridge - the oldest surviving bridge in Newcastle.

62. Shields Road
Look carefully and you will see that many of the buildings are the same in both shots. Notice the bay windows of the pub on the left are the same in both photographs.

64. Walkergate
The two pubs are the same and some of the buildings on the right of the old photograph remain today.

65. Armstrong Bridge
The railings to the right of the house are the link.

66. Blue Bell, Jesmond Vale
The pub, the bridge, and the houses in the distance are the links.

68. West Road / Slatyford Lane, Denton Burn
The link between (a) and (b) is the white house on the left. The link between (b) and (c) is the post office on the left.

69. Fox and Hounds Pub
There is no link here.

70. Benwell Village
The link is the building on the left which is now a bed centre.

The Tram Accident on Westgate Road in 1891

Other books by Geoff Phillips

Tyneside: Past and Present

Over 100 photographs of Tyneside as it used to be alongside views of the present day. Intriguing facts and information about each photograph along with a descriptive journey around Tyneside which shows the reader the views in the order as they appear in the book.

Price: £6.95   ISBN 0 9522480 0 X

Tyneside Pubs: Past and Present

Tyneside Pubs: Past and Present is another book in the hugely successful Past and Present series. It presents the reader with a nostalgic pictorial pub-crawl through time and Tyneside. More photographs from the Jack Phillips Collection show pubs in Newcastle and its suburbs as they were in days gone by along with modern photographs showing how things have changed. A pub quiz is included to test the reader's knowledge of bygone boozers.

Price: £6.95   ISBN 0 9522480 2 6

Old Pubs of Newcastle

A collection of photographs of pubs from the past.

Why remember old pubs of Newcastle? For many Tynesiders the pub is their second home, a place to unwind, a place to hear a good story or joke, a venue for a dart's match, a forum for an impromptu discussion on any subject under the sun. The pub is part of the culture of a town or suburb; a sociologist wanting to study a town's ethos might visit a pub for an instant picture of the townspeople's attitudes and way of life. Pubs also form part of the history of a city, its architectural heritage, its styles and fads.

Or maybe its just a place to enjoy a canny pint and a bit crack with your mates.

Price: £4.95   ISBN 0 9522480 4 2

Newcastle: Then and Now

Earlier books by Geoff Phillips have mainly featured photographs of Newcastle upon Tyne and Tyneside as it was in the late 1800's and early 1900's. This book compares Newcastle upon Tyne today with a time that many people will remember; the 1950's and 1960's. As in earlier books, there are nearly always links between the old and new photographs. Sometimes these links are very hard to find which adds to the enjoyment of the book.

Price: £6.95   ISBN 0 9522480 5 0

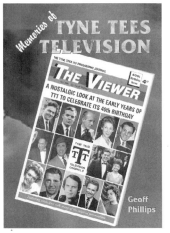

Memories of Tyne Tees Television

A nostalgic look at the early years of the North-East's regional television station to celebrate its 40th birthday

The book 'Memories of Tyne Tees Television' is mainly about the 'Black Brothers Era' (1959 to mid sixties) when Light Entertainment was 'King' and the City Road Studios buzzed with music, singing, dancing and comedy. The book includes many intriguing stories about the programmes and the people and features interviews with Mike Neville, Bill Steel, David Hamilton and many more personalities.

Price: £9.95   ISBN 0 9522480 6 9 (All prices include postage and packing)

All books are obtainable where you bought this book, or by mail order from G P Electronic Services, 87 Willowtree Avenue, Durham City DH1 1DZ